BETWEEN ANGELS AND DEVILS

JOHN CASTAGNINI

"Between Angels and Devils," by John Castagnini. ISBN 1-58939-850-5.

Published 2006 by Virtualbookworm.com Publishing Inc., P.O. Box 9949, College Station, TX 77842, US. ©2006, John Castagnini. All rights reserved. No part of this publication may be reproduced, stored in a retrieval system, or transmitted in any form or by any means, electronic, mechanical, recording or otherwise, without the prior written permission of John Castagnini.

Manufactured in the United States of America.

DEDICATION

Nothing has been a closer connection
with God for me than my poetry.
My mom's recent passing shattered my mind,
engulfed my heart, and enraptured my soul.
This book is dedicated to
the most special place my pen can find,
my mother, my light, my home.
Mom, I love you,
I love you more in every day
and with every breath.
Thank You.

BETWEEN ANGELS AND DEVILS

Between Angels and Devils

Although I see the perfection in life's love,
I cannot terminate the compassion inside
for the overwhelming illusion of injustice.

John Castagnini

This pen brings me to life,
but can my words kiss the world?

I see the perfection that does not make
the excruciating pain of life wither.

John Castagnini

<u>*Chance*</u>

Only gamble on the little things.
The brink of insanity will surely accompany
you through the big ones.

Between Angels and Devils

I may seem distant,
but that space is our closeness to become.
All the doubts that you see in yourself are minuscule
compared to the love and compassion that I see in you.
Our will to become love together is second to none.
You are the only security I have to build what is
most important to me,
my family.

I love you for you, who you are,
but most of all for standing beside me
as I explore the road in becoming.
A place I have always wanted to share
with you.

John Castagnini

We are all one in a billion

<u>Important</u>

The more important I become,
the less important I become,
the more important I become,
the less important I become....

John Castagnini

A Snail

I sat here today with a dream,
pleading please come faster.
A snail's at my feet. I scream
suddenly sensing its laughter.

Each patch of grass welcoming it
drifting on top of each blade.
I match the ass in hurrying shit
wishing to stop the dreams I made.

Its fluidity oozes compassion
beyond the stupidity of passion.
As I sit right here and ration
to bond divinity with what I fashion.

Between 0 and 2

I have this notion.
We're more than particles in motion.
Deep like the ocean,
But more like a magic potion.
More than just fish and water below
Only the magician will ever know the show.
If you expect to find it all between 0 and 2
You'll bounce your head forever and never find a clue.

John Castagnini

Thought

An ant crawled off the tips of my fingers
and fell into the pool I stretch beside.
Tiny little whirlpools spun it in circles.
It escaped each vacuum, only to be led to another
eventually enveloped by its ocean.
And though its struggle ceased, it remained
spinning to deeper waters.
A moment ago wandering at the tips of my fingers,
an anteater's dream.

Untitled

An ocean's breeze
sets the palm tree leaves to life.
Two trees side by side extend
their branches toward one another.
The trees dance, they dance in the wind.
They nestle, retreat, and then extend again
with what seems to be a yearning to simply touch.
I am no more than these trees
simply because at will I might tear them
from the earth and apart from one another.

<u>Untitled</u>

When the dreams I yearn for
unite with the dreams I see through your eyes,
life sings.
We create your song, my dance
only when I listen.

<u>Vortex</u>

The sunlight glitters upon the ocean
as if a cluster of a million shooting stars jamboree.
A vortex, a passage to the depths of the sea,
somehow spiraling through my soul.
My eyes open to the sky.
I gaze at the sun. Squinting I see a little bit more.
A cloud hurried to save me.
Droplets of rain caress my skin.
I'm alive.

Poetry is sharing
where the world and I
find our secrets.

Between Angels and Devils

I am alone with this page,
and it is all right.

John Castagnini

My Why Woman

My why woman,
what should I say?
We found a key
and you're locked away.
As sure as I'm breathing
I'll swear these feelings.
But can you believe me
with all that is so?

You search for why
that I'm just learning.
I search for how
with a heart that is yearning.
We're both here turning
to each other to grow.

My why woman,
show me a way.
My why woman,
what should I say?
Bound by illusions
make this a start.
Heal the confusions,
open your heart.

My why woman,
I can list forever
the softness inside,
the smile in your eyes,
the little girl pleading
please love me so.

16

Between Angels and Devils

My why woman,
I'll leave you never.
I just can't hide.
Show me the whys
I'm lost here pleading
Please let me know.

John Castagnini

Untitled

Become the path,
and you will create it.

Between Angels and Devils

I'm told poetry has two homes.
I see the recurring story,
pompous haves and martyred have-nots.
And I am to choose for whom to write.
The haves accepting the facade
of erudite scholastics
and the have-nots griping,
rebelling with the ways of the world.

I'd rather write and read my poems
for me and the children of tomorrow
than cater the songs of my heart
to appease either.
Read me only if open to another of love's ways.
Both of your shunts birth the genius of one another
and I marvel speculating in between.
What gives one liberty is poetry.
Cater to your heart and the world will buy
instead of to a bunch of wanna-be their way
pseudo-thinkers.
A true poet is a position-ist in the quest to drive
the way to
position-less.
Welcome, true poets.

"There's no money in poetry."
The publicists, advertisers,
publishing houses, distributors,
editors, printers, media
and their big buildings seem
to be doing just fine.
Screw you, I am the poet
and I will be paid.
As I sit here watching a swarm
of bees tender to the impatient flowers,
I marvel at the honey they leave behind.
Sweet, like the nectar, the poet's words
nourish the heart and mind of man.
I thank you all, but I shall sip the honey too.
You'll see.

A Cave

A cave, a hideaway.
I am sheltered
away from the sun,
safe and cool.
I'd rather take my chances
and burn into the night.
Maybe I could perch upon the stars
shooting through the sky.
At least I get to know
a bit of who you are.
Burn me to tears
through all of my fears,
a million light years.

Untitled

Again, I gaze at the ocean.
Another thousand shooting stars
glitter in the sunlight of the water.
I rock back and forth to the beat of music.
They continue their jamboree.
But they follow me from right to left,
up and down, like a puppet on a string.
They are mine. Thank you.
They are me.

Cement

Thank God for cement.
As I glaze from a hilltop overlooking the Pacific,
here my mind unites the waves and sky at the horizon.
It is only my city that allows me
to cherish this freedom I now see.
Beyond the walls I call home
the palace before me is possibility.
And the earth in front of me
entangled with heaven
becomes less than a fantasy.

John Castagnini

Untitled

I gazed above only to find an eagle soaring.
It looks down, folds its wings, drifting to me.
About two stories overhead,
he extends his wings
and swoops even higher.
He looks down, folds his wings
and drifts to me.
About one story above,
he extends his wings again
and soars even higher.
Maybe this time, he will land by my side.
Instead this time, he hovers over me, and I wonder.
Is he admiring me from afar
or planning to shit on my head?

Untitled

WONDER

Untitled

God creates the probabilities
as I create the possibilities
and change the probabilities,
creating other possibilities.

Fear of the Furrow

There is a place where the high tide storms
over the rocks, and on the other side
forms a pool of nature.
It's filled with fish of a thousand colors.
A tiny furrow through the rocks is
the only way back to the ocean.
Even though mostly seven feet deep, at the furrow
the sea is barely an inch deep.
The tiny fish sputter through the furrow back home.
Three big fish won't fit through the furrow;
the water is too shallow they believe.
They approach and retreat over and over.
If they followed their tiny friends
they would only skip above the water for a moment.
But instead they wander aimlessly in circles
hoping some miracle will wash them to the other side.
I whisper, "don't fear the furrow." Sometimes
the little fish will lead you home.

John Castagnini

Golden Chalice

Your cup is full,
and my thirst quenchless.
Simply a sip from your golden chalice
nourishes me and I become more.
I'm alive.
You become the blood to my heart.
Your river empties into my sea.
Inebriated,
another sip, another sip.

Limiting God to simply acceleration
denies the possibility of infinite imagination.

So much,
Right here.

Between Angels and Devils

The best way to see
is to look through the mirror,
beyond the reflector,
through the guiding light.

With tenacity decree
today your eyes open wider,
through light burning brighter,
beyond each blinding fright.

John Castagnini

The true poet says the very most
between as few words as possible.

Forbidden Flower

What should I share?
Could she even care?
I don't reveal
I won't squeal.
Flower, come here.
Our hour is near.

Knotted between,
united I've seen
the rope of acceptability and
the hope of possibility.
Imprisoned, to sit and ponder.
Destined, we fit, I wonder.

Spin

Which cog
from the log?
Whose wheel,
I choose to feel?
You churn.
Whose turn?

MY MOTHER

All you are to me, you will never know.
There is not enough paper in heaven to list it.
Simply know that my will to become one with the
heavens
through life's most difficult tribulations is your
greatest gift.

This rock I build upon
in order to speak with God more every day.
It is the incessant tenacity I harbor
allowing me to twinkle, one day shine,
eventually bursting into stardust.

I appreciate this will more than anything.
It brings me closer to now
and gives me the strength to hurdle every fear
impeding
my path to a greater understanding
and a more profound experience in living.

John Castagnini

No matter a ceiling half painted,
dust covered sheets,
millions of letters scrambled upon the floor,
and within the sky
my heart beats on,
and the sparrow sings.

USA 2000s

You're under investigation.
Your thoughts are against regulation.
Words of liberty, a violation.
Your tongue hung in strangulation.
Just a number to the nation.
Don't give to the temptation
not to bend over for taxation
or you'll crawl in desperation
and beg for your salvation.
Forbidden wealth accumulation
In the name of securitization.

Forget about creation,
or risk mental castration.
You're condemned to isolation,
a total abomination
to life's inspiration.

John Castagnini

Somewhere between the snail's dreams
and the dragonfly's day,
I meander.
Discovering how,
Wondering why,
Uncovering now,
Just passing by.

Robin

You flew away
and I am left to wonder
where you are,
and what to do
with this empty cage.

John Castagnini

Love eludes u
as much as you fight it.

"You can try and change everything around you.
Until you change to DOING the priority WORK,
you'll just keep chasing imaginary dreams."

John Castagnini

People all have dreams
and no time to get lost in yours.
Share a light to their rainbow
and there you shall find your pot of gold.

<u>Sprinkle</u>

This ravenous beast
beats my untamed heart,
pouring love and passion
through a spout that appears
much too small.

John Castagnini

Living

When what you see isn't what you are seeing
and what you hear isn't what you are hearing,
then how you feel extends beyond your feelings.
Now you are on the way to experience living.

Seek

Insane, I continue to study?
You are all
and I'm almost nothing.
You are always,
I'm a flash forgotten.
In the end you certainly win.
Yet I persist in the illusion that
understanding and experiencing a little
more is all that matters.
An inspired healthy habit,
a senseless delusion of displacement?
Flip a coin.

John Castagnini

Nothing matters more,
than the poems I explore.
I plead make them more.
Naive, I implore
as if someone's keeping score,
opening another door
in God's retail bookstore.

_We_

Sometimes I forget
the deeper I indulge
the closer I become.
Sometimes I remember
the closer I become,
the further I wander from
who I am supposed to be.
Between forgetting to remember
and remembering to forget, are we.

John Castagnini

Spider's Web

Silk in the shining sunlight
passers-by suddenly captured.
The wind and rain pass through you.
Barely visible,
You sit on top and feast,
in the web you weave.
They come but never leave.

___Looking___

The more you believe
that you know what you are looking for,
the less likely you are to find what you are looking for.
The less you believe
that you know what you are looking for,
the more likely that what you are looking for will
find you.
What I am looking for
might be what I am looking for.

Love this useless quest?

Between Angels and Devils

My sperm, my tears,
maybe my blood.
Definitely not my dedication.
How about my music?
Certainly, my heart.
To blind eyes, deaf ears,
and a frigid heart,
does it really matter?
Or does it matter more?

John Castagnini

There really isn't any way to
arrange these letters to make me
understand.
Oblivious, infinitesimal, meaningless,
a better puppet naked begging at
God's hand.
What I am dealt appears ridiculous
pathetic, deranged
as if there really existed a sin.
I only ask for whatever it is that you
supposedly do
to let me love in the days that begin.

Between Angels and Devils

No words are less or more an idea
begging to be proposed.
Whatever a man is to become or be
is whatever he supposed.

A rhyme screwing confusion,
taunting deliverance, imagining my hour voiced.
A time disguising illusion,
contemplating transcendence, laughing by our choice.

Stuck feeling tortured by the kingdom
more helpless than helplessness,
with humility whispering, bleeding,
condemned and convicted
to the probabilities to which I'm forever bound.

But hiding beyond wisdom,
emptier than emptiness,
with futility screaming, pleading
imprisoned and engulfed,
by the impossibilities of a switch never to be found.

John Castagnini

Fuck the rhymes.
Sometimes a break is what's needed.
It's simple. I'm furious, distraught,
lost at how to come to terms
with a blame,
full and bleeding.

It's OK to just pretend I guess.
I guess anything is really OK.
I only pray my mind can change course.
Because if it doesn't
I'll surely become insane.

Yes, Mom.

It makes me furious
at what has happened.
Furious that you wanted to leave us.
Furious that you wouldn't listen to me.
Furious at myself for my shortcomings.

Yes, I need to work this out
and figure what it's all about.
I know how to.
I just hope with all of my heart
I can do this.

John Castagnini

<u>My Way</u>

My way is mighty.
It's sensitive,
tender,
full of appreciation
and compassion to understand.
With a single hope that this will lead my heart
to share greater love
by developing a mind with greater understanding
of who we are
and how we might dance in the skies.

<u>Heaven</u>

Most people won't ever reach heaven,
because they follow the rules too well,
imprisoned by the illusions of a haven
casting an impenetrable shell.

Interrogate Me.

Do I recite the profile
where you imagine love hiding?
You want what you wish me to be.
I'd rather follow the flame,
igniting one another beyond the
fiery facade, burning into one another,
two hearts' naked truth.

Fill Me

Longing for connection to the vibrant oneness,
only this essence allows us to be the dreams
of the heart.
In sharing we become a soul of greater inspiration,
of greater dominion.
We imbibe the tears of the Goddess,
our chilled hearts fill.
Through our veins she feeds our tenderness.
So when we speak,
be sure to inhale the fragrance,
nourished by the soul of a
grander, deeper more profound love.
I am.
We are.

John Castagnini

When you're making up the stories
and you're not telling anyone,
you are their brain.

Between Angels and Devils

Every moment is worth
exactly as much as you let it be

The best poem
can never be written.

Between Angels and Devils

Nothing serves more than
the few words in between
the answers when listening

John Castagnini

A true poem
can never be written

Between Angels and Devils

I'm just a man lying on a bed
looking at the ceiling.

Sure, I believe in God.
I just question him.
Ridiculous?

Wrong Number

I've been calling.
Of what use?
No one was listening.
I've begged to please
come inside.
I found a place where no one
can hide.

John Castagnini

I figured a poem
would help me.
For the first time, I'm stuck.
I see no way to share
the scariest place
I have ever been.
Now, I understand why she left
this torture.

Between Angels and Devils

A single way to the soul
turns into a new way every day.
Life's dedication detours us.
Only when we leave, pretending
beyond the only truth, this moment.
With a little luck we get to
share one more moment than we hoped for.

John Castagnini

Allow the will
of who I am to guide
and remember its
subservience to the
will of what's to be.

Move On

The rules judging poetry, I intend to explore.
The fools praising history, they defend and implore.
A most vivid picture for everyone to see?
Or a livid fixture, where no one can really be.
A form and a rhythm is a must to be extolled,
Perform in a prison, I'll bust before I'm sold!
A need to write the mind directions is the simplest of
thrills.
But to lead plight to find expression is the greatest of
skills.

John Castagnini

**Greater**

How deeply I feel would surely scare you so.
I am a man making dreams begging to show.
No doubt, I barely fit into the rules that exist,
like a rhino, ramming ahead with only a choice to persist.
All that really matters to me is to see and share one.
In all that I breathe, think, and say, in all that is done.
I doubt I can love you the way that
you need.
I can vow only love in every thought, word, and deed.
Sadly I know it might not be enough soon one day,
But my love for you is beyond any words I can say.

Whisper

The breath of your gentle whispers
beneath my wings
guides every ounce of existence through a secret kingdom.
It hides beneath the forest,
every branch another step on the ladder to this palace.
Whisper to whisper,
gently whisper.

John Castagnini

<u>My Way</u>

My way is mighty. It is sensitive,
tender, full of appreciation, and compassion to understand.
With a single hope that this will lead my heart to share
greater love, by developing a mind
with greater understanding of who we are
and how we might dance in the skies.

Yearning

This aching, this yearning,
the gift of infinite learning?
Surrounded by people.
Can't escape being alone.
Even with the love of everything,
I contemplate the journey to nothingness.
Every breath a gift,
filling the emptiness with all that
the fulfillment emptiness can comprise.
And there am I.
Why?
Because you call everyone, I choose to listen.
Why?
Because I am nothing.
Why?
Because I rule ONLY how much I let
myself understand.
Why?
Because your beauty is all that really matters.
Why?
The obsession to know you is who I am.
Why?
Because I know I will never find,
but here is where I can hear more, even if it's a
single note, every time I listen.

John Castagnini

I Asked

Be careful what you ask for, so it is they say.
I simply asked for the deepest love to lead my every way.
I found a few majestic moments sailing me to heaven
and a torturous patch in between asking this
devilish question.

Between Angels and Devils

You're passing through my mind.
Can I leave it all behind?
You're deep within my heart,
a quench, a perfect start.
Please don't let my fear
prevent you from coming near.
Knowing the only promise I can make,
if I finish this poem, my heart will surely break.

Love
Kill
Smart
Love
Cum
Wealth
Love
Fuck
Caress
Love
Heal
Dumb
Love
Chaste
Poor
Love
Intimate
Rape
Love
Ovle
Rvlo
Love

Which Way to Go?

Greater decisions, we eventually face.
This blasphemous love we slave to,
needs we crave, people we cling to.
Awareness of this futile quest
obligates me towards jolting toward
and obliterating away from the insatiable
desire to love, to conquer love,
to love in conquering. I am free from nothing,
except to accept my slavery to everything.

John Castagnini

Die now, why not?
Why not go in a moment
of glorified triumph spawned
in a moment of a puzzle completed.
An endless problem with infinite conclusions.
Imagining forever,
one extra piece and one piece missing.

Between Angels and Devils

So here we are this conglomeration of thoughts,
feelings, dreams, hopes, pains, aspirations,
ruling ourselves with laws, morals, religions,
expectations, guilts, and fears.
And for what?
Part of me wants to just throw this pen down on
the floor, but the writing persists.
Why?
So we can organize this humanness into a way.
A way to what?
A way to someone or something that guides us? A
way to what we think will build something,
something grander, we believe.

Ignorant of the continuous transformation, we
place value upon the perception and conviction
towards our "evolution".
Our evolution towards what?
Becoming a greater peon certainly doesn't inspire me.
How grand can a peon ever be?

But my pen persists because somewhere inside
there's a way, a way to something deeper. Maybe a
facade, I doubt that conveniently. Maybe I doubt
only to give this meaningless life some kind of
meaning. I consistently might learn, see, and be a
greater ordered perception. But in a universe so
grand how can this mean evolution? Any
evolution to infinity sounds insane.

Maybe one day I may see. I doubt it. But, maybe.
And the only guide I shall accept is the one heart

John Castagnini

sharing a deeper more profound way of sharing
the love in my heart.

A deceptive delusion of grandeur. A fate of
inevitable nothingness. I imagine like everything
else the truth lies somewhere in between.
Though I might seek the former, privileged and/or
possessed,
my pen persists.

Between Angels and Devils

I am tearing apart a bridge to my heart,
drowning in the ocean below.
Gasping for breath I imagine a raft,
better yet a luxury liner.
Destination unknown, forecast stormy,
But still I can climb aboard,
imagining this tour is to a cherished wonderland.
The gift of ignorance,
the delusion of grandeur.
Not to escape, but to surrender to the possibility.
Deeper unification,
Spiritual stimulation,
Mental tantalization
to greater trials and tribulations.

John Castagnini

You may never know
how deeply you touched me so.
You'll imagine that our parting
was the result of hearts departing.
We simply love in different ways.
I regret my ignorance in many days.

You're a being I deeply cherish.
Our Love will never perish.
Many of my dreams are for yours to come true.
It's tearing up my heart, this path of leaving you.

But we both must grow in our own special way.
My heart's with you through every single day.
I hope one day you'll appreciate and understand
and squeeze each dream in the palm of your hand.

Between Angels and Devils

Confused and alone
I roam a palace.
I'm lost in it.
Shivering inside, condemned at every turn,
I wonder, I wander.
Can I ever find a way?
A way to where is a much better question.
I pray for this way.
This blame can surely drive one insane.
Needing help,
while knowing you can help yourself is a paradox.
Once found, it follows every breath for a lifetime.

I've lost any comfort
in being right.

Between Angels and Devils

Be strong willed,
but not overpowering.

Allow a little leeway
but not an open highway.

Be silent and listen,
but not solitary and ignorant.

Hear both sides,
take only your own.

Be the leader
by surrendering to follow.

Few love the net
where they choose to be captured.
They mostly forget,
dreaming beyond exists rapture.
This net, the glue to hold my life together.
Ignorant, I'm engaged beyond the comfort of its
pleasure.
Within our caging, another net, found strapped
even steeper.
Like moors raging, a better bet, bound trapped
even deeper.

Between Angels and Devils

You made the locks,
You own the keys.
My only key is nonsense.
You'll turn that too, only
when you wish.

John Castagnini

Running up and down,
the football game upstairs,
a whore on the net,
stuffing my face with potato chips.
There is nowhere I can get.
Covering up this frown,
climbing those stairs,
I hope to be set.
Stuck inside this place,
stuffing potato chips in my face.
Somewhere I can forget.

Between Angels and Devils

Screw Schrödinger.
No should of, could of,
or would of
will bring her back.
I never opened the box
and she's gone.
Thank you God for
leaving me alone
to appreciate my
ignorance in the
Murder of my mother.
I thank you with all
of my heart so very much.
Truth is you're not to blame.
You gave me the answers
and I chose how to use them.
Thank you for the blame.
The rule maker, I guess,
shares no blame in the
universe he rules.

John Castagnini

I found a penny today
and picked it up.
It looked ancient.
I thought it might be valuable
so I put it in my pocket.
I read the date later that day.
It was 1990.
Throwing it away, even spending it
would get me nothing.
How much more valuable it would be
if 100 years older.
Maybe then it could be
worth thousands.
So valuable, I would certainly
save it.
Well, would selling it and sharing it
then get me its value?
A worthless penny today,
I put back in my pocket.

Between Angels and Devils

Every road is
less taken.
No Road is taken more.
Each with a different destination,
Leading to the same place.

John Castagnini

The more strongly I once believed
in something, the less I eventually
needed to believe in something.

Between Angels and Devils

The more I knew of God
The less I knew of God.

and

with greater appreciation for the present
I become the greater presence.

MOM

If appreciating the illusion of
your leaving will allow me
to appreciate your real presence,
then I will commit to this.

With my life's dedication being
to understand what is,
I must know this transformation,
not merely wish for it.

Hence, I will see the perfection
when I allow myself to see the perfection.
I trust only you to guide me.

Between Angels and Devils

As long as our fulfillment is found
in the presence of an evolution,
discovery will appear as recovery
and the admission to appreciation will
appear as love.
Our presence is
our evolution towards presence.

Our greatest wisdom is
found in discovering our
greatest ignorance.
Our greatest love will be found
in admitting this ignorance
through appreciation.

Between Angels and Devils

The same bullshit
that we swear with putridity
gives game to the forest
in bearing fertility.

John Castagnini

___Filling___

Enough about me,
Allow yourself inside.
Maybe you will
ravish this world before you.
How shall you share?
Does a morsel of you even care?
It's simple to resist, easy to
remember a life of dreams missed.
If you'd investigate, interrogate your moments
you will certainly entrap the bits of your
wisdom to reveal _(Fill in the blank)_.
This excruciating pain and blissful
ecstasy will guide you. Only you can
decide how often you visit.
Are these bits worth it?
I too, sometimes wonder.
But once you fill in the blank, nothing
will become more important. Your answer
may appear to change. Eventually
you'll see how infinitesimal our lives are.
Every breath blows even GOD almighty
beyond a word or way. Separate, but whether
we like it or not you'll find this blank that
you fill, the emptiest craving, but you'll be back.
We will find each other there.

Between Angels and Devils

For a second I will believe
in complete possibility.
Every other approach might have
spewed the answer.
My deafness and blindness prevailed.
Make 2 loves one?
Mold them into an answer.
It appears to choose one.
The magic of this page!
Here I can turn two into one.
Maybe an angel will make this more than a poem.
Eventually I'll appreciate Love's choice.
For now, I'll appreciate God's greatest gift,
Imagining and this page.

To decide upon a soul
which dream to build.
Love's choice begging to
topple the pillars erecting my mind.
A being who'll follow.
A being who'll unite.
The greatest leaders
are the greatest followers.
I yearn to live that gifted role.
Follow a love; open a way more
difficult to understand?
A partner who carries part of the way?
Thank you for this wondrous choice.
I can certainly kill you for the torture
of this extraordinary position of futility.
Help me honor the killing and be gracious
with your gift, this choice, and whoever remains.

Windshield

Today I ran over a pigeon,
He was supposed to get out of the way.
I stopped for the children to cross
as the high school girls peered
with temptation and wonder.
A world through my
windshield.

John Castagnini

I'm screaming in your ears.
Stuck it right in your face.
You chose the tears,
You lose the race.
Thank you for now,
Is that all you can say?
Thank you for now
Always headed my way.

Allowing a way I sort of believe in
to fade away isn't much easier than
imagining who I believe I am to
suddenly disappear.

Ladies
The truth is that most of us,
most of the time,
have absolutely no idea
what to do with you.
Wear this, say this, look here,
don't look there. We're lost
and we don't want to take directions.

Between Angels and Devils

A young lady bellows at the loss of her first love.
A young couple tortured by the doctor's fatal
sentence on their first born.
A young boy, unemployed, wonders from where the food
for his two young children will come.
An older man wonders what to do for his long
days, shortening in retirement.
An old lady worries each day more of her back away.
A young woman opens her heart for the first time
to trust and love.
A young older man wonders
through the loss of his first love.
One day later that same
young man's mom passes.
A much older man is he.

John Castagnini

<u>My heart</u>

It beats, it pumps.
Sometimes it appears to open.
At least, I wish, I think.
It dreams, I'm told it loves.
I'm told it keeps me alive.
My only hope, it surprises me
and one day becomes my home.

Life is what you believe
you are going through
in what you believe
you are getting to.

John Castagnini

Believe it or not,
It's right in your face.
But blind as a bat
You'll miss its grace.

My life's quest?

Spilling the blood that nourishes my mind
From life's divine heart,
Through the ink of my pen, with love
Through the warm breath of my lips.

John Castagnini

I once believed in causes too.
I had my pointless point of view.
But life went on, no matter who was wrong or right

Billy Joel

THANK YOU

John Castagnini

In Loving Memory of
LORRAINE CASTAGNINI
January 9, 2005

You're still now, but still our mother.
We thank you for being exactly who
You wanted to be, our mother, our family.
Even through the pain of this passing,
We hear you, our mother.
Thank you for being the love that
Glues us together, our mother.
We will go on thanking you forever.
Our hearts are truly one,
And we will remember that always, our mother
We will use your will of love
To bind us even tighter.
You're beyond us now, yet with us even more.
We love you, we thank you, we pray for you.
We will cherish you more in every day to come.
Thank you mother. Thank you mother.
Your family, your friends, we thank you.

www.ingramcontent.com/pod-product-compliance
Lightning Source LLC
Chambersburg PA
CBHW021341090426
42742CB00008B/692